ONE DAY
I AM A FIELD

BY
AMY SMALL-MCKINNEY

GLASS LYRE PRESS

Copyright © 2022 Amy Small-McKinney
Paperback ISBN: 978-1-941783-84-9

All rights reserved: Except for the purpose of quoting brief passages for review, no part of this book may be reproduced or transmitted in any form or by any means, electronic or mechanical, including photocopying, recording, or by any information storage and retrieval system, without permission in writing from the publisher.

Design & Layout: Steven Asmussen
Cover art: © Rudolf Vancura | Dreamstime.com
Author Photo: Janie Glatt

Glass Lyre Press, LLC
P.O. Box 2693
Glenview, IL 60025
www.GlassLyrePress.com

One Day
I Am a Field

CONTENTS

The Doctor Said We Need to Return In Two Months After Further Testing Including Bloodwork	1
Clematis Vitalba	3
Saying It, At the Art Gallery	4
In the Near Dark, Gratitude	6
The Scan Revealed A Lacunar Stroke, Right Thalamus	7
Breath	8
Noir	9
Devotion	10
During The Pandemic You Are Dying At Home	11
Grief	12
Grief	14
A Woman Named Grief	15
Grief	16
Grief	17
Thirst	18
Grief	20
Poem Beginning With Lines From Rumi	21
From a Dead Father to His Daughter	22
Again	23
One Day I Am A Field	24
Hallows	25
Apple Crisp	26
Grief, Two Parts	27

Recurring White Form Against Black   28
Love/Furious   29
Before the World Ends   31
Without—   32

Notes   35
Acknowledgments   37
About the Author   39

In memory of Russ

*and placed my grief
in the mouth of language,
the only thing that would grieve with me.*

Lisel Mueller, from *When I Am Asked*

*

*I did not know the work of mourning
Is like carrying a bag of cement
Up a mountain at night*

Edward Hirsch, from *Gabriel*

The Doctor Said We Need to Return In Two Months After Further Testing Including Bloodwork

How do I mourn a husband who sits beside me?
Who cannot remember

doctor or diagnosis.
Who called me *Honey*, held

my hand. I could have held him
all night, woke to memory, the word dementia.

I cannot close my eyes or hide.

Who do I tell?
What do I need to remember?

My shoulders are mountains
where a shepherd must stop,

her sheep hesitating then moving upwards.
They hate the dark.

What to remember?

On the top of the mountain
not a burning bush. A woman, ruins.

Below where sea stifles land
my body a sunken ship, its ruins.

I am drowning in remembering.
In *memorari*, to be mindful of.

I don't want to be.
Want to forget alarms

for medications, cups of water to be thickened
so he doesn't mis-swallow into trachea or lungs.

Forget legs as stems that barely hold him.
Not-remembering is venomous, a stonefish,

unnoticeable, unremarkable at first,
easily mistaken for polished stone.

My shoulders are his mountains.
I don't live in the mountains, never a shepherd.

My city has its own steep cliffs of loss.
This city where I walk two blocks for apples.

When the emergency dispatcher demands
who is with him the man on the floor—

he remembered to push the emergency button.
We are on our way.

I am not a mountain or shepherd or sea,
I'm on my way.

Clematis Vitalba

There must be a way through
but all I know to do is throw
my white dishes rimmed with blue
orchids across a room
until all that I have is broken.

Except for one self-sufficient succulent,
I don't know how to make anything live.
There must be a way
but I don't know how.

I want to bury myself inside the dark. Stand inside
invented light. While the world falls apart,
my husband's brain swells with lakes.

Pink roses that sprawl across the apartment
building's metal fence don't need me. I'm not
the caregiver of blossoming.

Grief does not ask me
to be *pretty*, does not ask me
to be a corsage pinned to a gown.
It wants me to push up from roots
that scarcely survived, enter
its plain door.

I want to push my husband in his wheelchair along our rutted
road as though Traveller's Joy— *Clematis vitalba*—
scrambling a lattice fence to flower next year.

Saying It, At the Art Gallery

after Eileen Goodman, Tumbling Clementines

A shadow, across orange clementines tumbling out of their bowl
asks the right question. One clementine, left behind, swears: *I have nothing to say.*

But where is she, the artist?
The pine crate slightly left of the light, she might be
the shadow lifted on elbows or the mouth, magenta & opened.

~

Later look out our window at the black locust, how it turrets
behind a milky shade that limits light and dark,
& the tree is separate from & we are separate from.

Except I want to tell you how my husband refused to kill a red ant
because an ant's antennae are bent like arms at the elbows, because it might have family,
he really did say, then ferried it out on his gigantic finger.

~

& how within limits of light & dark
I am still mother, sister, lover.
Do you think it ends?
Vagina, breasts, the body as porringer, *a bleeding bowl*?

~

Know this: The words are not leaving or left or if.
The words are: I will look for him,
his scent of magenta, the red of his ant.

~

Fact: Clementines are seedless if grown in isolation.

~

My words are seeds.
If   when   leaves   no   apart from the other.
My mouth, red & hunted.
I have said it:
When he dies. When.

In the Near Dark, Gratitude

For long grass with purple tips.
For thin sweetgrass braided like hair.
For not falling, a curb's refusal to accept an errant shoe.
Thank you for these legs. The origin of a hum from bile and ash into
almost-belief.
For these minutes I move toward grasses that move toward me
into a breeze that hasn't learned the silence of my new country.
My country, I, fighting for its life.
Against despair. Its constrictor-knot, no-music no-sun signing for help.
For long grass, Purple Tears, sheared back.

The Scan Revealed A Lacunar Stroke, Right Thalamus

Where Can I Look
to not see you

My Window Is Not
a hand cupping the resilience of water bears

The Black-Capped Chickadee That Flew Into It
refused it

First Let's Talk About
a curve of impractical light
a pitcher to pour it into your body

except   *I Want*
to burn away everything

This Is A Secret
will I ever be loved again

None Of This Matters
helplessness follows me for spare change

I see you

Breath

Music on the vintage radio
as falling leaves stopped in mid-air.
Air revealing itself for the first time
as a body or a car leaving a driveway.
Air knows what is worth waiting for
and what is not.
I want to be air
wait with brilliant patience unafraid.
If this doesn't make sense look
out the window as air waits for snow.
I know it as air knows snow.
As a body knows air when it cannot catch its breath.
If able, every day we breathe in at least sixteen kilograms.
This is not wisdom.
This is eating boiled eggs buttered toast
food reassuring as snow.
Animals need to eat, true?
Need to breathe the oxygen in air.
Don't conflate air with oxygen. That's a mistake.
We also breathe in its poisons—too much kills.
That is the problem with air
and with love. I don't want to live
without either. I mean,
it is impossible.
What is beautiful about air
is how it helps to move water from vapor to ice
to sublime again, almost like music. Holds my love
as he tries to go from couch to table and back to couch.
Knows he will be ice and vapor. What we all become.

Noir

My mother cried on her satin pillowcase.
I never knew why, want to move toward her
wherever she is, ask what darkness
she could not crawl out of.

There are things I will never know,
though she told me:
I didn't hold you enough, uncomfortable with touch.

When my daughter was born, I held her
as a cloud holds on to rain as long as it can.

Now my love, on spoonbill legs,
ribs butting out against skin wafer-thin,
unlocks his mouth when he naps,
beaking for words lost to him.

The painter Pierre Soulages
said black is never the same
from morning to afternoon
to night and morning again.

Like my body,
dressing and undressing
in the dark. I put a hand
over my eyes until light
lifts me toward another body,
its leaves falling from branches.
It's ridiculous we are not trees,
though I want to be.

And since skin on skin breaks open all sorrow—
no—a turning away or fear of becoming
him, I don't hold him enough.

When no one is looking, I will walk
into the painting, thick black shoots,
unfastened trees in search of light.

Devotion

     Last night I moved into another room as I move toward becoming
a guest in my own life.

     Our daughter was born just before my body closed. Her father wore face paint—
characters in plays they acted out together. Danced in the living room to Springsteen
feet on feet.   How it was.

     Last night I moved into   became a guest in my own life.
A stranger, no longer my home.

He fell again this time in the trash room.
A neighbor lifted him using a fireman's hold.

Later he could not sleep. His body
fire-cracking open   hour after hour.
His body a baffled tornado.

     Last night   moved & I left the room listening
for boom or crack or breaking glass
trying to sleep
trying to remember the love poem—

                This must be.

DURING THE PANDEMIC
YOU ARE DYING AT HOME

Sparrows nibble at your blanket
dive in and out of the eaves of your mouth.

Wings rimmed with tatting.
Tattooed beaks add color to an otherwise

bland room. The hard-working birds
will not speak to me yet.

This is not the life I planned.
Now the sky closes its doors and trees shrink

into fetal positions. Your body shrinks.
You forget where you are where

you are going. Your hospital bed tries to explain:
You don't belong anymore.

This is not the life we planned.
We are breezeless our window won't open.

I wait with the sparrows for a sign
to kiss your confused mouth goodbye.

You say:
    "I'm moving three across three down."
    "What if my pee is poison?"
    "Get me my shoes."

Grief

> —You were going to go without me? That was always your story.
> Jean Valentine, *The Messenger*

Learning to roll and remove pee-soaked sheets from under a body isn't easy. Sometimes, I pulled so hard, you screamed out. To calm you, I used my motherly voice, stroked your forehead. The human body as dead weight. The body unable to stand or walk or lift itself. Reason and home disappearing. You were at the bank. You were reading rental ads. You wanted to be certain we'd live somewhere safe. You were not in our bedroom anymore. The shelves on the other side of the room that hold photos were not shelves. You told me, "I am moving three over and three down." Or pointed to a photo of your dead parents and told our daughter, they are playing pinochle. You told our daughter the exact number of your bridge masterpoints but insisted you still could walk.

*

There are things about dying I didn't expect. How the dying stop pissing and shitting and then suddenly whatever is left inside is released, flung out like birds from a rotting cage. How the dying will stop breathing, then a gasp again, open their eyes, then no breath, finally. It must be what is meant by taking a last gasp. It must be what is meant by birds on a wire before migration.

*

I keep telling you to come home, enough is enough. I wake in the middle of the night afraid, sleep with a light on as I did when young. What am I afraid of? Aloneness does not have a body. It does not have a gun. It cannot creep beneath the door frame. Still what I see is a figure, a man, and he is moving in and out of my room at night. It is not you. Were it you, I would not be afraid. Maybe I need to open my eyes to the comfort of your dark. Not yet.

*

I dreamed our clothes fell out of a massive closet, and he was there
to help. Shirts are scattered across his closet floor, and I am alone.
It feels exhausting to place them, one by one, on wire hangers. Wrinkle-
free, cotton, flannel, still here, with me. I imagine little birds nesting in his
closet now instead of moths. I imagine the toxic moth balls are snowflakes.
Sometimes I am handing over tax forms; sometimes I live in a forest that is
red and yellow and trees chattering to themselves. Then
I return to the accountant and the lawyer and the fallen shirts. All I can do.
Shuttling back and forth between nests and concrete, metal and leaves.

*

In the car today, I asked you how I looked in my dress. I told you I don't
want to live without you, and you took my hand. Air has its own shape. It
is solid if you know where to look. It opens its doors if you know where to
walk in. This is the place I love most.

Grief

> I am poling my way into my life.   It seems like another life:
> *Jean Valentine, La Chalupa, the Boat*

Nothing to stand on but cotton balls. A child would call them clouds. Floating in a summer pool is not enough. Water demands a body right itself. I have lost control of my body. Will I die from caregiving and grief? A friend died six months after his wife. He didn't listen to the screech owl inside. Summer calls for me as though I understand. I am listening; she is speaking in tongues.

*

Two ceramic angels sit on my bookshelves.
I am an origami owl, turned inside out.

*

Why did my husband die in summer? His favorite tree finally bloomed; I love its light colors blending with the dark. Gingko, I want to lift you from your roots, lay you in my bed, but you would die there too. I couldn't depend on you to tell me how the world is doing without him. When you seized during the storm, I knew to cocoon myself inside the throw decorated with red and grey cardinals and lie on my couch as though a stone, the one I'll place on top of his grave.

*

As always, you wanted to row beyond safe buoys. Russ, remember the boat we took out at Cacapon? As always, I said no, we can't. Life is dangerous. My body, a frozen lake. My body has stopped being summer. I am afraid, if summer, someone will drown.

A Woman Named Grief

Removes his name from bank accounts,
signs documents, mails certificates of death.

Buys a new rug, he's not here to trip
and fall. Its unruly swirls

remind her of roses.
Cobalt blue, mint green, muted reds.

She is not muted. Crimson, furious,
held together by helpless leaves.

In the night, beetles eat away at her roses.
In the morning, the damage is clear.

Grief

refuses to take a nap
or look out the window
at the ginkgo tree that gains
and loses its leaves
long after the others
or later at the wobbly moon
so insanely determined.

                I cannot ask
it to go away though I thought I could
as if that were enough.

What if I cannot find the synonym for alive?
What if and if nothing forever in one room, one.

Grief

My body is a blade. Nothing to annihilate but the Self.
My body refuses to sit still. Rocks back and forth to its own deafening vicious silence.
I know how to laugh out loud.   Everyone thinks I am fine.

Mouth as river-vein   after all
returns blood to a heart.

Thirst

I will use this pencil to draw you back to me.
If not to this world, then inside, rising
like a river or bones Ezekiel brought back to life.
Never a conclusion, always imagination's axle
rotating in the wheel's center.

This is not about Ezekiel, exiled to Babylon,
his crazy visions almost hidden from the canons.
This is not about Ishmael
who lived to be one hundred thirty-seven, child
of Abraham and Hagar.

Hagar, a mere handmaiden to Sarah, chosen by Sarah.
Is this about a slave purchased to carry a son?
How the seed grew inside of her, how
the seed grew like mastika sapping from a tree.
A tree becomes a forest of believers.

How Hagar and Ishmael, forsaken, were dying
in a wilderness, until an angel showed
her the well, the angel
reclining by her, O for the thirsty.

O for you, my beloved, who did not live to one hundred thirty-seven,
yielded to fluids cresting inside your brain, pushing
against its walls, until there was no memory,
body and memory drowning in your own terrace of fluids.

Terrace, in Old French, rubble, in Latin,
terra, earth, akin to torrere: to parch, to thirst.
When you were dying, I used an orange sponge
to dab ice onto your lips.

How EMTs had come and gone so many times
to lift you, we brought in the metal bed, its locking casters.
No more sirens, except the one calling to you.

Yes, this year is over. Yes, I etch absence—
in grief's desert, I wait for Ezekiel to find me.

Grief

I walk from room
to room
as if
a pressing task
requires attention.

Then leave that room
for the next
and the next
to return to the first.

Nothing: any space I enter.

Except old socks missing
their mates
and whatever I need to imagine.

I cannot do this alone.
Then his hand obscured—
nothing whole—

Poem Beginning With Lines From Rumi

Don't pray to be healed, or look for evidence
of some other world.
There is no other. Here, we are here,
ground cracked and tender.
A blade of grass a mouth.
Even a broken body
in another room
still sees the moon.
Even you, in your bed alone, a moon.

From a Dead Father to His Daughter

Light lost in the mathematics
of unknowing.

Still,
you know still

where to look.
I am not the sky.

Not under the mat
by your front door.

Notice the songbird's feathers,
how they reflect invisible light.

Again

I can't stop thinking that/

I will never swim again
I have unlearned the strokes
that keep my head above water
       you held me above the wave
while you sunk below   knew
I was afraid that I am afraid
of everything   out there

I can't stop thinking that/

the sycamore you loved
by our window will
smack into the glass that protects
me now that you are gone   that I am
a gold-yellow leaf   a leaf   falling
into the dumpster below   into
guilt and confusion

I can't stop thinking that/

I will wake tomorrow   not a leaf
but a bear   a weary bear
wandering into
the wrong world   searching
for a stream
       I crouch over my cub
hold her   she will not drown

One Day I Am A Field

Instantly, soundlessly, a meadow called bereft.
        One day, a hawk's meadow.

Above, a red-tailed hawk fools me
into thinking he's an eagle
flaps his wings wildly

then glides until I know, yes, it is you.

What is remembered when blinded?
Try to wake to the sun's flash of denial.
        The problem: I am grief's land.

One day, I am a hollow.
        One day, a long depression of land, a hollow, carved out close to a river.

You bring me rain, carry it in your mouth
as if I were a baby bird. You make many trips.
Squat beside me.
There were never enough words between us.
Before you leave, you cover me with birch bark.
You are safe.

What I want for you:
        To be a Mountain Bluebird, escaping the blazing forest,
or if you prefer,
        water running downhill stretching into a river.

Hallows

And when the hectic light leeches upward into rolls of dark cloud

When all I want is to shut the door or wear a mask
to face it. All I want is to reveal
what is inside. Not red leaves, this pandemic,
a woman in love. But a sliver of autumn. One

of its dreary days when leaves are soaked and scattered. One
of the masked waiting for something, maybe
All Hallows, which I know nothing about except

children and nightmares parade in floats
or inside red wagons dragged by mothers or fathers.
And like one of its leaves, hang on, hang on
as though my life depends on it when all I want is to rely on

the small wagon of promise. I will fall my darling into my own arms
because you are not here, you are something like wind,
something like the angel asking for treats, something
like autumn air holding me up, midair.

Apple Crisp

I drove to an orchard to pick the last of
autumn, most having fallen beneath

or beside their trees. A cashier handed me a bag
to weigh what I carried back to her.

Signs pointed to the paths
I could walk or not, varieties I could pick or not.

Sun Crisp, Sundance, Pink Ladies, all that remained.
The path between the tree lines was straight, clear.

If I looked down, I pitied bruised flesh,
half-wolfed bodies of diminished fruit. If I looked up,

higher than I could climb with the nearby ladder,
a few hung like red bodies of winter cardinals.

Something safe about the paths, instructions
on what is alive and what has died.

Every night, I clean
apples with bio-wash, slice

them into quarters, sometimes eighths, combine varieties
so that sweet and bitter mix. Sprinkle cinnamon and nutmeg,

a few lumps of non-dairy spread, handful of walnuts
or smother with oatmeal, then set the oven

to 350 degrees and wait. Since you've died, since this apartment's
emptied of you, I try to understand distance.

Surrender floats into the hallway.
My neighbor, Rosemary, asks if I am baking.

Grief, Two Parts

      To Be

I want to learn the train's language
how to make sense to the tracks beneath me.

How to hear the rhythm of wind speeds
or salt speaking inside the sea.

Does the sea listen to salt?
If I hear you, are you close or faraway?

      Listening

Um yes okay   I hear you   still
      & what if I do   I mean

what is that sound? Hum? Bear rummaging
      & lost   An alarm clock—time to let me go?   You decide

                                                   I don't know

Always insistent inside.

Recurring White Form Against Black

After Sophie Taeuber-Arp, Gouache on paper, MOMA

They look like small boats growing
unexpectedly larger
or white ducklings
or paper hats that might float away
an inexact symmetry
none of them perfect
like us sitting each
in her own chair
still we are moving
toward something
isn't that what stillness is?
breath before the world
begins again
love repeating itself
against a window
your reflection
in my own

                                        for our daughter

Love/Furious

Not so cold that I want to stay indoors.
Instead, that vacancy between fall and winter.

The sidewalk here is crooked, broken,
entire slices of cement missing.

To walk, it is best to look down.

I remember when I fell, my finger broken,
my palm thickened with tangled branches
that forced two fingers to bend as if looking away.

Since he has died, I have awakened to a body broken
more damaged than I knew.

The bones of my legs creak like floorboards. I can't find
the body I knew before wipes, pills, the save him, save him.

I didn't hear my body ask me to look up, look
at my mouth opposing itself, one side in a perpetual frown,
the other still stupidly smiling.

Why was the left side of my face shutting down?
My eye closing, its lid covering half of the pupil.
I did not see it.

Or is this the divide between seasons, a caregiver's sleepwalk, the I am and I can't?

I didn't hear my body ask me to look down, notice
the purple bruise on my calf, notice
the heavy wood bedframe I walked into.

I must have been helping him tie his shoes or button his shirt
or hanging on while he tried to stand.

Or is this the divide: loving/furious? afraid/furious?

I wanted to pour myself into his spaces.
I wanted to break from him like a rib.

How many selves fit into love's nesting?

Or is this a lie? Or rather, not the same truth for the woman, the I
now sitting by the file cabinet sorting through history,
deciding what to shred, what to save.

She listens to voicemail, I listen to his voice, over and over.

Before the World Ends

after Canoe Model 1851, British Museum

I will put on shoes
with cork soles
carry him along our tree-
lined streets
he'll be heavy
we will make it to the river
float in water not earth
not trench and stone
I want sun
in our mouths
as calm as seedcakes
him to drift beside me
into the night when even the gate
has shut behind us
time enough to become
two slight boats built
from paper bark
moored together
in parting

Without—

Where are you?
Bird or air? Cloud of ice crystals?
Or a random word like prayer repeated
as I check-recheck a locked door.

Want to believe in
grass's greener edges before they dry
left over busily fading
smothered in egret snow.

I am a blade of doubt
though I want to say *oh gorgeous*
want to say if the next song
is about love
I live another day.

Notes

1. Again: *I can't stop thinking that/* from Sarah Vap, "Winter" (Noemi Press, 2019)

2. From a Dead Father to His Daughter: *Notice the songbird's feathers / how they reflect invisible light.* Source Information: "Scientists also have learned that many birds have plumage that reflects UV light. …bird behaviors may be shaped by secret visual signals humans cannot see…", from True Colors: How Birds See the World, National Wildlife Federation July 19, 2012

3. Hallows: *And when the hectic light leeches upward into rolls of dark cloud*, from John Ashbery, Baked Alaska, "Hotel Lautréamont" (Knopf, 1992)

4. Poem Beginning With Lines From Rumi: *Don't pray to be healed, or look for evidence of some other world.* from Rumi, "The Illuminated Rumi" Translation and Commentary by Coleman Banks (Broadway Books, 1997)

Acknowledgments

Grateful acknowledgement is made to the editors of the following publications, where these poems, or slightly altered versions of them, first appeared.

Baltimore Review: "The Doctor Said We Need to Return in Two Months After Further Testing Including Bloodwork"

Fatal Flaw Un(Confined): "The Scan Revealed A Lacunar Stroke, Right Thalamus"

The Indianapolis Review: "Saying It, At The Art Gallery"

The Inflectionist Review: "From a Dead Father to His Daughter" and "Without—"

Life And Legends: "One Day I Am A Field"

National Poetry Month 2021 - 30 Days of Inspiration, Arts & Cultural Council of Bucks County: "Poem Beginning With Lines From Rumi" reprint with artwork by Nanci Hellmuth

One Art Poetry Journal: "Tending to Living Things (Clematis Vitalbe)" and "Breath" and "Again" and "During The Pandemic You Are Dying At Home"

Poetica Magazine: "Thirst"

The Plague Papers, an anthology (Ed. Robbi Nester): "Before the World Ends" and "Recurring White Form Against Black" and "Saying It, At The Art Gallery"

Psaltery & Lyre: "Poem Beginning With Lines From Rumi"

SWWIM: "Love/Furious"

With gratitude to my mentors and poet friends who helped me along the way: Sarah Vap, Alicia Ostriker, Judith Vollmer, Michael Waters, Mihaela Moscaliuc, Ellen Doré Watson, Afaa M. Weaver, and Sean Nevin. Thank you, poet Virginia Konchan, for your deep reading of this manuscript. Also, thanks to beloved writers Nicolette Reim, Irene Mitta, & Nicole Greaves for giving me the courage needed to finish this book. Special thanks to Catherine Bancroft and Alison Hicks who saw many of these poems in their earliest stages. And to my Montgomery County Wordshop Poets who helped me to chip away at the unknown, including Liz Chang, Grant Clauser, Hayden Saunier, Doris Ferleger, Susan Charkes, Tom Mallouk, Joanne Leva, and Sean Webb, thank you. And to the Glass Lyre Press Team, thank you for your generosity and commitment to poetry and your authors. I want to also thank my dear stepchildren, Adrienne McKinney & her family, and Rick McKinney for accepting and supporting me. To my son-in-law, Alex Simanglatt, thank you for loving Russell and watching the Eagles with him. Finally, to my daughter, Sarah McKinney, now Simanglatt, who always inspires me and reminds me of love even in the face of grief.

About the Author

Amy Small-McKinney is the author of two full-length books of poetry, *Walking Toward Cranes* (Glass Lyre Press, 2016) and *Life is Perfect* (BookArts Press, 2014) and two chapbooks, *Body of Surrender* (2004) and *Clear Moon, Frost* (2009), both with Finishing Line Press. *One Day I Am A Field* was written in the course of her husband's illness and dying during COVID. For the 2020 virtual AWP, she co-moderated an interactive discussion, Writing Through Grief & Loss: The Intersection of Social and Personal Grief During Covid. Her poems have appeared in numerous journals, for example, *American Poetry Review, Anomaly, Baltimore Review, Comstock Review, The Cortland Review, Inflectionist Review, Pedestal Magazine, Poetica Magazine,* and *SWWIM,* among others. Her poems have also been translated into Korean and Romanian, and her book reviews have appeared in journals, such as *Prairie Schooner* and *Matter*. Small-McKinney was the 2011 Montgomery County Poet Laureate. She resides in Philadelphia. You may read her previously published work at www.amysmallmckinney.com. She tweets @amy_smallmckin.

Glass Lyre Press

exceptional works to replenish the spirit

Glass Lyre Press is an independent literary publisher interested in technically accomplished, stylistically distinct, and original work. Glass Lyre seeks diverse writers that possess a dynamic aesthetic and an ability to emotionally and intellectually engage a wide audience of readers.

Glass Lyre's vision is to connect the world through language and art. We hope to expand the scope of poetry and short fiction for the general reader through exceptionally well-written books, which evoke emotion, provide insight, and resonate with the human spirit.

Poetry Collections
Poetry Chapbooks
Select Short & Flash Fiction
Anthologies

www.GlassLyrePress.com

www.ingramcontent.com/pod-product-compliance
Lightning Source LLC
Chambersburg PA
CBHW030140100526
44592CB00011B/976